Table of Contents

11 | Crisis

17 | Revelation

35 | Learning As I Go

47 | Catching Up With The Present

55 | Lessons Passed Along

101 | Life Lived And Loved

1 | Crisis

REHAB 101:

"Write About My Pain"

What day? What hour? What activities? What MOOD?

My pain is always different, almost always there, subject always to my interpretation! It began very suddenly in July of 1996. In those days, it was PAAAAIIIINNN!! Just brushing my hair or getting to the bathroom were major life events, and I lay on Ted's couch and waited while test after test was run by the doctor, trying to figure out why a woman who'd played golf on Saturday couldn't move on Monday.

By the third day, I knew I was wallowing in it, and the thought crossed my mind that if Jesus walked in the front door and said "Pick up your bed and walk," I'd have started whining at him, and that I had to start managing my attitude.

They tested for Lupus, and MS, and Carcinoma, and all kinds of terrifying possibilities, and my doctor finally told me it was rheumatoid arthritis, and I would have to get used to it. When my eyes teared up, he suggested possibly a rheumatologist could help, and a new journey began.

My best bet for medication required that I get a mammogram first, and after being called back for the third round, we scheduled a surgical biopsy. Six weeks later, the results were in. The biopsy was clear, and the focus returned to my arthritis. I began to build my medication level gradually, all the while popping aspirin and depending on my sweetheart Ted for food, moral support, and his fabulous refusal to give up. He walked me to the front of the house, to the house next door, to the second house, to the third house – took me to the driving range to hit 3 balls, then 7, then 10 – always insisting that I try just a little more than yesterday's accomplishments.

I remember the day I actually washed my car! It was like winning the gold medal! I started showing up at work for a few hours at a time, and my boss complained that seeing me in so much pain was just too hard for him. I snapped at him that I wasn't going to become an invalid so he could feel comfortable! (He has since died of cancer, one of my dearest people ever!)

As the medication took hold, I guess what has become the hardest part began – the day after day, month after month, year after year monotony of fighting with it. Some weeks I can play golf three days in row and feel great, relatively speaking. Then I can wake up a day later uncertain if I can walk across the room. The "on and on" of it is the part I have hated the most. Six years, almost, and trying new meds, and exercising (sometimes for 3 whole minutes!), and resting, and trying to figure out what I ate right before it got bad and analyze it and figure out and BEAT it. And accept it, and manage it, and watch my attitude, and NOT go river rafting or run 10K races, but go to Hawaii, or Vancouver, or Sedona, and carry my heating pads everywhere. Working, succeeding, getting promoted, having to submit the budget from home one year, using a cane when I needed it, and a walker when I needed it, and walking the Juvenile Diabetes Walk for the Cure (3 miles) 3 years in a row.

It was in my knees and ankles, then my breastbone, then my shoulder, fingers sometimes, wrist almost always, feet most lately. Pain all over so that when I need to turn over in bed sometimes I have to grab sheets and haul myself to a new position. Sitting in conversation with people and trying not to let on that electric shocks of pain are running up my leg, or my arm, or simply wincing and gasping and letting it be, and wisecracking about it that it helps to moan, don't mind me!

Two years ago I gave up my handicapped parking pass, and this year I had to get it back. We get extra courteous service when we travel, and people are much nicer when I carry the cane than when I'm just slower than they'd like but they can't see that there's anything wrong. But, when I'm walking with a cane they talk to me like I'm stupider, like talking louder to a foreigner. Homeless people are very friendly to me when I have the cane! Corporate people look dubious, as though there may be a faulty circuit in my brain. It's impossible to feel sexy with a walker, and difficult with the cane. Getting out of the couch at the end of the 10:00 news can destroy a sexy mood. Sometimes I feel ninety years old. Sometimes I feel like I am William the Conqueror, because I did something I wasn't sure I could do, like go Christmas Shopping! When I can hike a mile or two, or swim a few consecutive laps, or play golf, I feel like the happiest person on the face of the earth, because I appreciate it so damn much! I teased coworkers once that they needed something neat to happen to have a really good day, but all I required was getting out of bed without wincing.

Now I am applying for jobs, totally unsure if I'll be able to show up once I get one, but determined to try. My brain is just too damn good to do nothing. In'valid and Inval'id seem too close in my mind.

Pain in my body has made my spirit a bigger part of me, separated my identity from my body, taught me gratitude for the simplest activities, shown me how much people love me, inspired my friends, awed my bosses and coworkers, and given me a deeper spiritual life than I ever thought possible. It's taken all the fear out of getting old, because I really really want to get old.

Pain in my body has taught me that self-pity can destroy in me, and what projecting the future can create that Steven King couldn't begin to compete with. It has forced me to slow down and be still more often than I might do otherwise, required that I ask people for help, lean on my friends, and pray, pray, pray. I have been a success while in pain. I have led my church through an incredible conflict while in pain. I have laughed while in pain, and been a good friend while in pain, and cooked gourmet meals, and become a pseudo-grandmother to Ted's grandkids, and coached a childbirth, and written poetry, and sung beautiful songs. I've also whined, moaned, feared, resented, self-pitied and why-me'd till I've totally bored myself, drank, isolated, drank, cried, and lay awake at night wondering if it would get better enough by morning to show up for whatever was on the schedule. I've pushed people away, and then been terrified that they'd leave. I am constantly amazed that Ted still loves me after six years of this crap.

I have consistently refused any narcotic painkiller, and hope I will always be able to do so. I take my prescribed medications regularly and never cease to be grateful that there is at least something they can do. And I hope. And I get dressed, and show up, and so far, I've never stopped trying. I've come close! But I tried again. And I'm still here trying.

This has been one of my worst weeks, because I walked at the AT&T Golf Tournament in Carmel, and pushed past my limits and woke up in the nights hurting horribly. This has been one of my best weeks, because I was able to be at the AT&T, and laugh, and play, and eat wonderful meals, and go to meetings, and be Ted's partner, and share birthdays with Tommy Smothers and Alice Cooper, and hold a brand new grandson, and laugh and tease with the other three grandkids, and I made it out of bed every morning, and back there every night even though I was almost crying by the time I got there one night. That's what my pain is like for me. There.

My counselor listened with tears in his eyes. He said, in a choked voice, "You've reminded me of taking my two-year old to a fair. She was all cranky and fussy, and when I squatted down to console her, I looked around and realized she couldn't see the fair. All she could see were asses and purses!"

2 | Revelation

Baby, baby

Infant friend,
You lie there discovering us,
Uncontaminated with ideas and experiences,
Making no meaning yet, of it all.
It will come to you too, my friend!
Your imagination will grow,
Your opinions will evolve,
Your self-imagining will take its shape,
And it will all look real to you.
If you could only tell us now,
If you could only show us how
To teach you only beautiful realities,
To help you remember your spirit,
To express always the gifts you came to give us!
We have only our contaminated minds,
And our imaginings are real to us too.
Be patient with us.

PRINCIPLES FOR LIFE: A ROADMAP FOR REALIZING MY LIFE HAPPENING.

Sydney Banks, a man I have yet to meet, changed my life. A welder and a very unhappy man, Mr. Banks experienced and captured for the rest of us a spiritual epiphany, where in an instant of revelation he was able to realize his own mental health, and simplify his transformation into a description of three principles that govern all human psychological functioning.

The Energy that powers all life, our Life Force, if you will, he refers to as the Principle of MIND. Scientists tell us that we, and all that surrounds us, are energy. That this energy has a creative intelligence that impels it into form, then impels the forms it has taken to continue creating, may sound more like a science lesson or a recap of quantum physics than a map of our psychology.

When we, as creative beings, capture that life energy, we transform it through our second function, THOUGHT, into ideas. Throughout our lives we generate these ideas, first through instinct, intuition, and natural wisdom, and later through memory, analysis and making meaning.

As quickly as our thoughts are generated, without regard for the value or the accuracy of the thoughts, CONSCIOUSNESS delivers them to our physical bodies, using our chemistry to give us the experience of our thoughts as reality.

For my students, they know my 3x5 card version of the Principles: "The experience that I'm having today was created in me, through Mind, Thought, and Consciousness." For my friends, the earthier version, "Oh, that's just me, making s___ up again!" is more familiar.

I have sat, in the last six years, through hundreds of hours of classes, continually looking anew at how these three fundamental principles work together to create my entire life experience, yours, and our experiences of each other.

At the time that I was introduced to these teachings, I was suffering horribly from rheumatoid arthritis, and my life experience was dominated by physical pain and the grief and sadness I generated around the pain. In time it became clear to me that even a circumstance as direct and indisputable as the pain in my body was only transformed into my experience through Thought, and that the quality of the thoughts I was processing were far more important to my daily experience than was the actual level of my pain. Some days, my pain level was high, but I was in a happy, playful mood. Some days, particularly if I'd been doing well for a while and then my pain level escalated, I was immersed in self-pity and despair, having a horrible experience.

Another "circumstance" of my life was that I was deeply in love with a man who did not have good thoughts about marriage. My own parents had a very romantic marriage, and I had dreamed all my life of creating that kind of relationship for myself. I was constantly torn between breaking up with a wonderful person I loved, or giving up my "dream" in order to stay in the relationship.

As my understanding of the principles grew, it became clearer and clearer that I had created my dream from my memory of my parents, and was not being present for the reality of my own relationship. I found a new way to experience who he is, be who I am, and be part of the evolution of our relationship, which has become deeper, happier and custom-designed to the people who are in it, instead of the fantasy I'd blown up in my mind. Two years ago when he was having heart problems, I held his hand in the emergency room and our closeness was utterly tangible. I was hit with the reflection that I had searched all my life for this relationship to happen to me, and had never realized that you have to begin with a stranger and build it, one moment at a time.

As I have met life happening in the understanding of the Principles, I continually notice the role of my fantasies in all of life's struggles. It is virtually impossible for me to be upset about the way things are without having first created an imagined picture of how things ought to be. As my thought structures of resistance, attempts to control, and rebellion began to be "busted", my mind has simply become a quieter, more peaceful place to live.

I've developed a genuine amusement at the ways I generate my experiences, and can honestly say that I am enjoying my life.

After all, if I'm the one making it up, I can darn well make up something fun!

IT'S MAGIC!

In the very instant
Circumstance plays before me like a movie
My inventive mind
Makes meaning of it.
Looks into my memory,
Relates it to some other circumstance,
And knows that I know
What is happening.

In the very instant
That my mind "knows" what is happening
It delivers what it knows
To my physical body
And I begin to think I know
What made me feel
This dreadful feeling.

Like a baby
Making meaning of the bib,
Full of joy because there's food to follow,
I react to what you do and say
And make meaning of your motives,
Creating my reality anew
Every moment.

What a gas!

INNER WELL

In pain, I meet the Self of me, the one
Who hears the message, wears the body,
Is no part of inflammation,
Knows nothing of deterioration,
Except the message it sends.
When I remember, I become aware,
For the first time since the newborn
"I" discovered my toes, (back then when I was
wise!) that there is more to me than this fragile,
Imperfect form walking the world (or not).
There is a spirit
Totally well, totally healthy, totally young.
There is a spirit never lost,
Never baffled, never adrift.
Where has that spirit been?
Not lost, but buried
Beneath its own creative fluff,
Making up that its own created form
Was all there was.
And that it was a separate thing at all.
Writing scenes, playing them out,
And scaring Myself.
I spend Life making life,
Believing it is true.
O' Spirit found,
Remind me in this pain that you are well.
Remind me I am not these bones at all!
Give up your game
And let me know your Peace!
Oh no, my little being, on the game will go!
Your turn is not yet over, be Alive!
Be something new.
Be ME!

CREATIVE

The tree does Live freely —
Grows leaves; Flutters in the breeze;
Endures the storm;
Feeds from the earth and the sun.

The apple tree doesn't seem to worry
That the cherry tree is doing it all wrong
But I, being Life Creative,
Make up ways to fight the flow.
Make up meaning; make up trouble;
Make importance out of circumstance,
And ultimate importance out of
MY circumstance,
And supreme importance out of
Life happening as ME.

I have sought long and hard
To make meaning out of life,
And see finally,
Now that my turn is almost over,
That I was simply Life
Struggling with Life,
Absorbed in Life,
At odds with Life,
Missing out on Life.

LIFE HAPPENING

What I am is Life Happening.
What You are is Life Happening.
Life Happening Right is an idea we created.

The more I wrap myself around the Idea,
The less Life can happen.

Life took form as me.
Life took form as you.
The more I do Form,
The more I forget Life.

When the forms of life
Become the forms of memories,
We have a tendency
To see it as loss.

But then Life before form
With nothing at all missing,
Gives life to the magic
That Life never leaves.

When Life happening as me
Recognizes Life happening as you,
Right there, Right then,
Life is happening.

(for Jane)

LIFE AS ME

No more than an idea that Spirit had
To live a life as me,
I venture out upon the road
And watch to see the next horizon.
Now is rich,
Pushing me gently
Into discovery
Of the now ahead.
The open channel
Is not a habit yet,
But a novelty of joy and trust
That baits me forward.

JARROD

When he was a baby, he knew it all.
His eyes would look into you,
Clear to your soul.
They talked to you of great Wisdom,
And I knew that he knew that I knew too.

But so very soon, at three and a half,
He had learned of comparing himself about,
Wanting everyone's attention at once,
And knowing, but not liking, right from wrong.

I have seen his thoughts evolve
From the birthday
When everything had to be yellow
To the birthday when Purple was king

As he created opinions
And then new opinions.

I watched him shift
From the center of the universe
To being the brother,
Offended by the arrival of someone new,
Vying for the attention and stomping his feet.

And his self-image started becoming.

I watch him come to visit, and always flash
To what we did on the last visit,
And want to re-create the past
Because the memory was fond.
And I know I do that too.

I watched him learn,
And be appreciated for his intellect,
And start to know
That being smart was his gift,
And start to judge
Kids who didn't know what he knew,
Because judgment
Became a safety net in the
'How'm I doin?' game.

He'll be six this month,
My beautiful boy,
Still loving to cuddle,
But not to be seen cuddling.

Still challenging his brother,
But calling him to come and play.
Still becoming human
More and more every day.

CARMEL CONSCIOUS

Sitting on the beach
In Carmel, California
I note that every tree is malformed,
Beaten by the winds and time
They all stand bent and one-sided.
Yet standing side by side
They create one of the most beautiful
Landscapes in the world.

Like the likes of us,
All a bit battered and worn
When we stand alone.
We reach out for each other
And form Humanity,
A beautiful thing.

WHERE WAS GOD?

God was there being God all along.
All the while I was creating
Him in my own image
And delegating my wishes to Him
And being crushed that
My Way wasn't prevailing.
God was there being God
While I was seeing death
As the ultimate tragedy
Instead of the way of nature.
God was there being God while I
Was seeing illness as a personal affront,
Instead of the source of my greatest growth.
God was there being God while I
Thought unemployment
Was a personal punishment, and for a moment
That my JOB was my Source.
God was there being God, the Breath of Life,
The Quantum energy, the Intelligence.
Factory issued at a cellular level, and
Calling out for my attention,
While my God-given creativity
Was making up that I knew better.
Busy-minded, I wanted a God
Who managed my circumstances,
Immortalized my loved ones,
Blessed my finances,
And acknowledged my genius
For all the world to see.
There was God.
In the stillness.
Never what I thought.
Always more.

KNEW IT ALL ALONG!

A cell of life
Nestled in mama's womb,
Dividing and creating,
Knowing already what to do next
With native intelligence born
Before my brain was formed.
This Knowing never left,
Just got drowned out
By all the noise in my brain,
Making up ideas to struggle with.

BREATH OF LIFE

In that quiet moment
Just before sleep arrived
There was the breath
Where You inhaled
And I exhaled.

The breath of life
Where You took form
And Creative Imagining
Began the journey of creating one-ness
And forgetting Oneness.
And all the beliefs about Me
Became a structure
That limited my exhaling
You beautifully.

3 | Learning As I Go

Gridlock

On the freeway of my creative genius
There was a 62-thought pile-up today,
Causing intellectual gridlock.

Mental Mayhem.

Wipe out.

It began when one small memory
Sat down in the road
And escalated
When a memory crowd began to gather.
Analysis collided with retro-fit,
Nostalgia slid sideways into regret,
And remorse wiped out
An entire row of successes.

Not a fresh idea could get through.

And as old used thoughts
Were honking their horns,
Blaring for attention,
Losing patience with the chaos,
Intuition and Inspiration
Quietly moved to the side of the road,
Smiling their patient, knowing smiles,
Biding their time peacefully
Waiting for the normal flow to reappear.

It always does.

WITHIN

Where have you been? They asked.
I've been Within.
I've been in residence
Where seeking isn't called for,
And answers aren't missing,
And You and I aren't far apart at all.
I've been expressing the eternal force
Wherever Life is called upon to act as Me.
I've been where Wisdom's voice is loud,
Where needs are few
And Form is but a playground.
I've stood with Understanding.
Beneath the chaos I create,
And found Wellbeing where
Imagination stops preventing it.
I've lived in every now that's been
Since last we met.
Come calling soon.
You'll like it.

HEALING ALTOGETHER

To heal my circumstances,
I searched everywhere
For the right job,
The right home,
The right romance.
To heal my body,
I searched everywhere
For the right pill,
The right exercise,
The right food.
To heal my mind,
I searched everywhere
For the right book,
The right class,
The right attitude.
To heal my spirit,
I had to stop searching altogether,
Look within,
And await the glorious peace of acquiescence,
Spiritual Home,
Where circumstances and physical form
No longer appeared urgent.

PREMEDITATED STRESS

I made up a story this morning
About how my day should go.
I designed the outcomes I wanted,
And the people I wanted to know.
Then I saw the way things were happening
And the way people actually are,
And knew if my fantasies just had come true
We'd have all been happier by far.
They call it stress in the world at large
This resistance to what is so,
But I can't resist without fantasy
Of how I would want it to go.
My wonderful gift of creative thought
That imagines it all my way,
Sets me up for the fall when I'm thwarted
By an uncooperative day.
It is what it is and it ain't what it ain't,
My friend is noted to say.
But I want what I want when I want it,
And go struggling all the way.

WHO ARE YOU?

Looking out at you,
I create.
I see your actions,
Hear your words,
Interpret your expressions,
And imagine you
Lesser or greater,
Causing me grief or wonder.

Look Within,
I discover me creating.
You are another form of me
Expressing other aspects
Of the energy of us,
Doing well or insecure,
With no mandate to fit
My design of you.
In curiosity I can meet you
And discern what you create.

YAHOO!

Like a cowboy in the rodeo,
I circle my emotional lariat,
Taking aim at the horizon
Trying to rope my wellbeing.
Wherever it looks like it is today,
In that romance, in this job,
In a better place to live, a better friend,
A hobby, class, investment, oh.
All the places I can look
I see new targets for solutions
To the restlessness I made up
In too much thought.

I AM THE DIVA

I am the diva
Of all my mind's soap operas.
Creating dramatic effect
Where none is called for,
Adlibbing screenplays
When quiet would be more than adequate,
And filling the theatre of my life
With willful storms of expectation and passion.
Why would you think that I would be okay
With accepting things as they are,
Relinquishing fantasies and writer's privilege,
When I have been given this wonderful gift
Of Creative Genius?

CULTURED

Once upon a time
We all got together
And made up the rules.
And then we made them up again.
And then we made them up again.
And then we made them up again.
There's always someone,
Often me,
Who doesn't like the rules.
Are we the rebels?
Or are we the inventors
Of the next set of rules?

IT DOESN'T FIT

When I was little
I knew in my heart
I was a Jazz Saxophone.

I seemed to be surrounded
By concert violins.

I tried my hardest
To be a good concert violin
Because it seemed to be expected of me.

From my chair
In the center of the violin section
I had no clue there was a whole orchestra
Waiting for my tune to play.

DISCOVERY

The spiritual heart did not come in the doing.
In showing up for classes
And lighting candles
And reading endless books.
There I learned to think spiritual thoughts
Making new spiritual noise to add
To earth's chaos and my own.
I learned it in the vision of insight,
Creating different nows
Than I knew how to make before
Filling my world with our Creative Spirit,
Taking form here and there as me and you
In Its own image.
Creating us Creating.
Creating rules and culture and opinion,
Creating good and bad, and heaven and hell.
Expressing all We are all over.
And Life goes on, creating this and that
For us to play with.
A crisis here, a triumph there,
To wrap ideas around and build a day.
To wrap ideas around and build a life.
To wrap ideas around
And find our own way home.

4 | Catching Up With The Present

Chronic Attitude

I notice the fear
Of feeling like this
For the rest of my life.
I can feel this way now
And get through this day
But don't tell me it's an always thing!
I'll detonate.
Acting fine is hazardous to my health,
Although I am better at it
Than anything I've ever tried.
People ask "are you still in pain?"
I shrug.
I almost remember being without it.
My life was a model's stride,
Confident and sure, daring you to look,
Not caring if you did.
Today I am a hobble
Stepping tenderly and checking
To see if I made it through
This one next step,
Next day,
Next thought of how it used to be
Or how it will become.
I can only bear to feel this way
In the very now.

MORNING SONG

Morning blessed me with more today
Than the coffee and A.M. Show.
Today I woke up to the Spirit at play
I'm occasionally blessed to know.
I woke up aware of the Force of Life
That pushes my feet to move,
And shining afresh with the Light of Life,
That sits me so firm in my groove.
My heart felt full of the Love of Life
That bonds me with everyone,
And my mind was light with the Song of Life
Where the melody's never done.
I flashed for a sec on the sorrow
For days I don't wake up this way,
And a moment of fear for tomorrow
That the feeling I have may not stay.
But that is the trick of life's Spirit
Never missing but always hiding
In the totally present minute
Where my thought is seldom abiding.

MINDSTORM

Adrift in a sea of fantasy
With nary a cove in sight
I'm conjuring worst-case scenarios
And drowning myself in fright.
The waves of endless potential
For ways things can turn out wrong
Bat me around my emotional sea
With a current rough and strong.
I feed the ideas like honored guests,
And they settle in to stay.
I find no clear perspective
To shoo the illusions away.
It's a time when all that can save me
From a shipwreck of massive proportions
Is the point of view of a friend or two
To subdue my stormy emotions.

FUTURE TRIP

I've never done next week before,
It's all a mystery.
I struggle with it all the day
Creating fantasy.
Since there's no information
On the day approaching fast,
I look behind at what I know,
Collected from the past.
And finding nothing that can tell me
What the future holds,
Anxiety possesses me
Until the Truth unfolds.

Then I embrace the "I Don't Know"
That sits in front of me,
And realize the fantasizing
Isn't serving me.
Come back, come back, and do the day
That's here to do today.
Tomorrow's path will follow
And the road will show the way.

LIFE AS ME

No more than an idea that Spirit had
To live a life as me,
I venture out upon the road
And watch to see the next horizon.
The Now is rich,
Pushing me gently
Into discovery
Of the now ahead.
The open channel
Is not a habit yet,
But a novelty of joy and trust
That baits me forward.

REMEMBERING ANEW

Resurrecting old hurts
Was an area of expertise
Supported by an emotional library
Of mental video cassettes
In stereophonic anguish,
That could be called up and replayed
Anytime the insanity struck.
One by one they took reviewing
Not from the director's chair,
But as the comedies they were.
Not as weapons for use
In brutalizing my presents,
But as memories that saddened my past
And served as catalytic forces
To teach me to be who I became.

5 | Lessons Passed Along

Making Stuff Up

THE DIVINE GIFT

Imagination may well be mankind's greatest gift, but we can also see it as our greatest curse. With the knowledge of Mind, Thought and Consciousness as the Psychological Functions that deliver our reality from birth to death, we start to notice how much of the day we spend making things up, and how exhausting it is. Here are some examples of habits of thinking that don't serve us well.

Retro-Fitting the Past – From the day we are born we are accumulating and storing memory. That's our human nature. But we can create the habit of bringing those memory tapes out and replaying them repeatedly, forever imagining new ways that the past should have gone, what we should have said, or how much more caring and loving "they" should have been. The root words for resentment mean to re-feel. And as we re-think the past, we create unpleasant feelings, over and over.

Script-Writing the Future – Making plans is one thing, but enacting the future in our imagination continually creates worry, anxiety and just plain terror as we make up all the possible ways things might turn out. Letting things play out may sound like a tall order, but it's nowhere near as hard as living constantly in tomorrow.

Meaning-Making – In our interactions with others, only their behavior is visible to us. We can only guess at what they were thinking, and how the situation looked to them. And guess we do, forever thinking that we know exactly what their motives and attitudes were. When we realize we are making up all of that, we very seldom get our feelings hurt or take offense. If the phrases "people will think" or "I don't want them to think" are regulars in your self-talk, you are probably in the habit of making up a lot of meaning.

Speculating – When I don't know what's going on, I tend to make things up! A great thing to know about myself, because when I start getting scared by whatever I just made up, I can remember that I'm the creator!

"I don't know!" What healing words! I don't know what they meant by that. I don't know what is coming. I don't know why. I don't know what you are thinking. I don't know what was in my mother's mind in 1952! Wow! Now I can relax! Being able to know that I don't know frees up about 10 hours a day of heavy thinking. I can only imagine how I'll spend that time!

IT'S NEVER THEM!

I hate that part of learning about the Principles of Mind, Thought and Consciousness! If I'm feeling stressed, disappointed, angry, annoyed, hurt or abandoned, part of me would still love to see it as "their" fault. Blaming others for how I feel is a lifelong habit, but the privilege of the unenlightened. Usually by our third Health Realization class, it has begun to be clear that our experience of others has nothing to do with the others and their behaviors. We can ONLY experience our own thought about the other. Bummer!

Of course, the same is true for the good feelings I experience and "blame" on others, like romantic love, delight, affection and enjoyment. It's just as difficult for me to see that my grandchildren aren't the source of my laughter and the great day I just had, but usually we don't create problems for ourselves when we're mis-crediting our good feelings.

It's the aggravations of life that build into resentments and severed friendships, and when I'm deep in feeling that somebody done me wrong, sometimes the best I can do is remember that it isn't – it's never – them.

It is Consciousness doing exactly what Consciousness does, translating the thoughts that are traveling through my mind to my physical body's experience by way of emotional sensations. I think, therefore I rage, cry, scorn, fear and experience what will always feel like reaction to them. Consciousness is so efficient at what it does that I fool myself into thinking that what they just did caused the feeling I'm having. But, alas! Not so.

The proof is in the good moods, when all of mankind is less annoying, and I'm having no reaction at all to exactly the same behaviors. I can't even remember what it was that was upsetting me so last Tuesday! It isn't on my today mind! Or better yet, when someone I really like does the same behavior, but I find endearing and totally forgivable in my friend what was completely unacceptable in another. Oops! Busted. Of course, there is some comfort in knowing that I don't cause annoyance in others, either. But what if they don't know that it isn't me?

ENERGY MANAGEMENT

We hear a lot in our society about waste management and conservation of our natural resources. When we recognize that Thought is energy, transformed into form by us, we bring new meaning to the ideas about energy conservation and waste.

When we wanted to change old habits, it took lots of publicity and raising of awareness on the part of our government to create a new idea in our minds, like recycling, or to stop being a litterbug. Thought Energy is a much simpler resource. There is a natural resilience that lifts our awareness level and eliminates waste whenever we become open to noticing.

When I am in an easy flow of thought, I feel peaceful, present in the moment, and secure. But as my thought-speed revs up and I begin over-producing with my thought-energy, I slip innocently into my personal brand of thinking, bouncing from past to future, making meaning, and coping with what I've made up.

The first clue is that my body systems are accelerating, becoming busier. I can feel my heartbeat, respiration, and tension levels reacting to the increased exertion of Thought Energy. My mind may feel stressed, and I may be experiencing trouble sleeping, or focusing on what I am doing. Or, if I'm investing in anticipation or fantasy outcomes, I may be daydreaming or feeling impatient with the present (bored). Eventually my system will feel run down, fatigued, anxious or depressed. The feelings that accompany Thought Waste are my emotional dashboard, letting me know that the needle is in the red zone.

What to do? Trying to manage my thinking, or not think that any more, is like thinking about my thinking – it may feel better for a minute, but actually creates additional overload. Like bringing emergency vehicles to the scene of an accident, it can compound the problem, blocking the neutral flow of thought even more.

When I see the feelings I'm experiencing as what they actually are, a barometer reading for the quality of thinking I've been in, I am able to simply take the reading, respond to it, and intuitively adjust. When I'm truly clear that the feelings I'm having are feelings my own thoughts are creating, they simply aren't such a big deal. I'll create something else pretty quick!

SETTLING FOR LESS

At infancy, a newborn lives totally in the present. They quickly let us know of their wants and discomforts through their instinct and intuition, by crying. As we grow older, our perceived wants and needs are experienced as a sense of longing. We attach the feeling of longing to some item, person or situation outside of us, and become certain through thought that if we could just attain the Desired, all would be well. We pursue our "fix" to exhaustion, and if the perceived goal is achieved, we can often experience a sense of let-down after the newness wears off when we find that our dream come true didn't satisfy us as we expected. Alternatively, we experience enormous feelings of loss if it can't be accomplished as we desired.

Briefly, the dynamic looks like this:

- Clarity and wellbeing exist constantly in our innate thought, and never leave us, BUT---
- We become assimilated in personal thinking, losing our natural serenity
- We experience a sense of disquiet, and associate it with desire for ??? (we fill in the blank with some outer form.)

Then.....

- We achieve the desired and it doesn't fulfill us, OR we are unable to achieve it, and we settle for less.
- Discontent continues, and we identify a new goal.

Often, when we don't get what we want, we

try to fill the sense of longing with an alternative item, person or situation that we consider "settling for less".

With an understanding of the Three Principles, we know that our every longing is actually for that good feeling innate in us that is part of our clear and impersonal way of thinking. This Wellbeing, always present and available to us, is the true nature of what is missing for us when we feel restlessness, dissatisfaction and longing. While it has never disappeared, we can mask it with intense personal thought, and create a sense of lack.

Every person, place, thing or situation to which we assign our sense of longing is, in actuality, settling for less. There is no substitute in the world of form that will give us that same deepseated peacefulness and content that we feel when we are truly centered in the moment and seeing with innate, impersonal thought. If we are experiencing a sense of urgency, or it appears that our wellbeing depends on a particular outcome, we are still searching in our learned, personal way of thinking. We are still settling for less.

BECOMING THOUGHTLESS

Last week I misplaced my keys, and they were finally found hanging in the car's lock in the fairly public parking lot. For me this was a clear sign that my thought activity was "over the speed limit" and I was absolutely not present. It was a very natural offshoot of starting a new job, having to learn new tasks, new people, and even a new commute, and I was glad for the wake up call.

In the past, when being immersed in thought was a way of life and totally unconscious, I've been known to become accident prone, exhausted, or obsessed with food without the benefit of insight and awareness. This time, I was able to adjust my routine a bit, get a little more sleep, eat especially healthy, and "wait for the fog to lift."

Multi-layered thought, whether recognized or unrecognized, can lead us down a myriad of undesirable paths. Depression, mania, insomnia, panic attacks, addiction, and a full menu of health problems can result when our minds are unable to quiet down to a smooth, natural pace. Distraction, forgetfulness, accident-proneness and restlessness or boredom are more benign manifestations. Whether it is appearing in my outer picture as workaholism and superstardom, as perfectionism and being all things to all people, or as overwhelm, exhaustion, or one of my myriad of "comforting" addictions, it is all the product of a thought-manufacturing plant that is in overdrive.

I can reflect on childhood experiences where I was in exaggerated fantasy, the anxiety of wanting to be liked and trying to compute what would please everybody, and even the years of obsessively climbing the corporate ladder, and see that I did not form this habit accidentally. I pieced it together methodically over most of my lifetime.

So I've created this habit, what do I do now? Remarkably, the mere act of recognizing that I'm mentally speeding, thinking in high gear, is often similar to noticing that I'm speeding in my car – there's an instinctive slowing of my pace. But the real advantage of knowing that I'm speeding is in the acknowledgement. If I'm distracted, it isn't a good day to make decisions, dump my feelings on others, or become self-destructive. It's better to fasten my seat belt and wait for this particular part of the ride to be over.

IT ISN'T THERE!

My client was having major anxiety because her history tallied a number of failures at creating a drug-free life, and she did not see how the future was going to be different.

I suggested she look in her purse, and see if she could find a $100 bill. She looked baffled, and of course said there was no sense looking there, as she knew there wasn't one.

It's the same thing to search the Memory for a successful plan for a new way of living! The more she searched in memory, the more discouraged she felt. When embarking on something one has never done before, acknowledging that I don't know what this is going to look like is a great first step. From there, we can begin to access Wisdom for guidance, reflecting on what our barriers have been in the past, and really listening to the keys our Guidance puts forward. We can also ask or watch others who have some success in this area, make a plan that incorporates staying connected to our Health, and venture forward knowing we are plunging into unfamiliar territory.

When we realize that the new territory is only unfamiliar because there is nothing in memory to assist us, we can easily reach in other directions for our help, instead of panicking at the sense of void.

When I first learned about the Principles, I

was on Disability and had lots of quiet time. The more I recognized that my reality was created in Thought, the less chaos I created, and my thought life became much quieter and more peaceful.

As my physical health returned, I found a job and prepared to return to the work world. Not knowing what it was going to be like to work full time and take care of my health as well, I intuitively knew that my thought life would become busier in the work world. I would be accessing my intellect, skills and becoming busier, and I felt fear that my newfound peacefulness would be lost. I was led to set up a schedule, and to include at least one activity each week to help me remember my new-found way of being. I committed to this schedule for at least a month, and the routine became such a blessing that I continued it for several years.

The habit of looking to memory for a sense of the future is learned, and we can become so entrenched in the habit that we have forgotten there is another way to venture forth. Curiosity about what this experience is going to be like, reflection about how I can best proceed, and the awareness that my Wellbeing is present, wherever and whatever, will give me what I need to do the next right thing.

WHO DO YOU THINK YOU ARE?

Just exactly who do you think you are? We say these words to each other to call each other down, or to put each other down, but the question can also be a real one. Our Self-Image, or more to the point, our Imagined Self, flavors every day of our lives.

From the time we are leaving our infancy behind us, we are beginning to look around us and create ideas about how we measure up. Remarks from parents and friends, siblings and teachers are noted and stored, with no understanding that they, too, are in thought. When situations occur around us, our magic little meaning-makers see the situations as having meaning about us. We piece our memories together like a mental mosaic into our picture of who we are. Over time, our picture becomes so real to us, that if someone says something that doesn't fit with it, like a compliment about something we see as flawed, we are unable to take it in.

A few years ago I had the opportunity to vacation with my family of origin. We enjoyed each other enormously, but I noticed that the activities I was choosing were frequently not aligned with the rest of the family. When I came home, I told my friends, "I figured out why I grew up feeling like I didn't fit in. I don't fit in!" I was able to see us on this occasion as different from each other, with nobody being wrong. Plus I was able to see clearly how as a little girl, whenever my opinion didn't fit everyone else's,

I had taken it to mean that I was an outcast. It was like letting fresh air into the attic of my memory, and so many of my old insecurities just disappeared in the breeze of insight.

In most of today's therapy models, with the best of intentions, we are trotted back into our memory bank to examine each piece of our mosaic and gain understanding of how the mosaic became the picture that it became.

With understanding of the Function of Thought and the storing of memory, in an instant we can SEE that the picture is a self-created illusion, and it disintegrates in the realization the "Holy ___! I made that up!" followed closely by, "I can make up something else!"

Or, even more exciting, I can abandon my comparisons and self-judgments, and simply be alive in my life. Without the sack of self-perception I've been hauling around for so long, and the calculating and maneuvering it has required to live with it, there is every possibility I could truly enjoy myself.

I CAN RELATE

When asked what we should talk about in tonight's session, the response is almost always Relationships! There seems an eternal quest to get it right in our relationships, and to resolve our romantic struggles.

In all of our relationships, and with our romantic partnerships, we can only experience another person through our own thought process. Often the breadth of the gap between the person themselves and the "person that we have designed in our minds" can determine our success and satisfaction in the relationship.

We start out fresh. We meet someone, and there is nothing about them in our Memory, so we are present and curious and eagerly getting acquainted, and the feeling that is delivered by being present is wonderful, so we decide "this person makes me feel good."

The trouble starts almost immediately, as we begin creating our own personal fantasy about the other person, an image in our minds of who we think they are, as well as a collection of memories about who they were the last time we met, and an array of imaginings about our future together. By the time the first three months have passed, we are often so committed to our imagined persona that we are missing clues constantly that would reveal their true personality. When behaviors don't fit our picture, we tend to dismiss the information as irrelevant, or feel disappointed and betrayed that they aren't living up to the expectations we ourselves created. Now when I'm with the love interest my mind is so plagued with expectations and insecurities, it becomes impossible for me to recapture that "fully present" feeling, and since we credited them as the cause of the feeling, we credit them also for its lack, and figure we must be falling out of love.

There is no word that has been more valuable to my romantic relationship and all my relationships with others, and that is the word CURIOUS. When I can remain curious about how my partner is thinking, I find we are continually creating that "present" feeling in each other, and the feeling of love goes on.

LISTENING IN

When I took the Core Course for Health Realization, we did a Listening exercise that totally changed my life and relationships with others. In pairs we tried listening to each other without drifting away into our own memories and personal thought, and for the first time in my life I realized how little actual listening I do!

As my partner was telling her story, I was "relating" with recollections of similar events in my life, "imagining" how she must have felt, "formulating" my responses, and "waiting for my turn" to talk. After the initial insight we tried it again, and what an amazing difference not just in my ability to actually hear what she was telling me, but in her reaction to my intense listening. We connected at a whole new level, and for me, my communication with others has never been the same.

I still have a natural tendency to roam around in my own head while people are talking, but I have learned to catch myself and "tune in" when I do.

My job at the time was in customer service, and I had dozens of calls every day from people of a wide range of ethnic and cultural backgrounds. I found that when I could focus on what they were telling me, I not only heard the words they were saying (even though often heavily accented), but I was able to hear their fear, their frustration, or their anger from a place of true understanding, and then was able to respond as their ally and helper instead of as an adversary.

In the evenings when I got home from work, I started looking at my sweetheart and listening closely to what he was telling me about his day, his health, or whatever, with the conscious intention of hearing what he was telling me. And lo and behold, he would stop what he was doing and listen to me as well! Our closeness began to deepen, and our friendship grew as well. We began to be much more inquisitive about how the other was feeling about life and people. We began to laugh more.

When I hear comments about our culture being self-absorbed and overly distracted, I see it now as just bad habits of listening. Even the cultural admiration for "empathy" turns us back within to our own reflection on how someone must be feeling, instead of actually listening to them tell us how they ARE feeling!

So listen up! Come to the present moment, and shut off your memory for just a moment. There may be something new there to hear.

I SEE YOU!

My friend called last night, crying after a phone conversation with her sister, who could not see that she had changed. It occurred to me how many times in a week I do the same thing with my family members and friends. I have a full data set on each one, and know who is likely to be late, who cannot be trusted with secrets, which ones are not reliable for lending my books, and who will only eat vegetarian. When one friend tells me she is seeing her old boyfriend again, I am known to roll my eyes in disbelief, knowing that they "always" end up fighting and breaking up. When another friend cancels our plans, I "know" that she's been drinking again.

It is as if my memory has an entire string of post-it notes attached to each name, and I have affixed the notes with super glue so that they never fall off. In effect, after I have categorized them, they have no means of escape from my assembled judgments!

What if I could use the experience data, and still remain curious about the people my friends are becoming? What if I were open to a new experience of them each time we meet? If one of them makes an effort to change a bad habit, wouldn't it be grand if I actually noticed! Once I have bound someone to their past behavior in my mind, I have totally abandoned any hope of having an actual, present moment experience of them. Our friendship is an ongoing instant replay, and if I am unaware, I am forever having relationships with people who no longer exist!

Of course, when I am judgment free, totally in the moment, the clarity of my thinking may also serve to deliver common sense observations. I will see people as they are, without making classifications – without seeing their "imperfections" as being about me, and discern the right way to be with them (or not).

The gift of being a present-moment friend is that we are free to bond and enjoy each other every time we meet. When I am seeing the other person through screens of memory, it is like looking through a very smudgy window – there is no clarity. When my screen is clear, my state of mind is grounded, every meeting is one of curiosity and discovery.

WEIGHTY MATTERS

What's your TPM? (Thoughts Per Minute) What we really need is a dashboard gauge that shows us the rate at which Thought is speeding through our system. When I'm simply cruising, and consciousness is bringing to my experience a passing flow of thought, I can comfortably move about the world, shifting gears into Common Sense and Wisdom, noticing life unfolding, and feeling fairly light in my emotional TQ (Thought Quotient).

But upsetting thoughts are likely to gear me up, and my thinking can feel like it's speeding out of control, before I even notice it's happened. Many of us are so used to habitual mental travel at high speeds, we are incapable of restful, peaceful meandering, and feel at a loss if the world isn't moving at warp speed as well. We dose ourselves with double lattes or worse to try to get our world aligned with our inner speed. But we physically pay the price for habitual speeding, and innocently we may perpetuate the problem until we have reached an emotional breaking point.

The "speeding ticket" will appear in many forms, including depression, anxiety, panic attacks, manic episodes, fatigue and exhaustion. We may look to the outside world like workaholic perfectionists, drama queens, or couch potatoes. But internally, the one word that always seems to fit is "heavy". We are carrying the weight of too much thought, often judging ourselves for feeling as we do, creating even more thought on top of the original malaise.

The slang phrase "lighten up!" would seem to apply, but when we're weighted down it is usually impossible to see the path out. Fortunately, the simplest solution to being revved up is very similar to physics. When we notice that we are accelerated, and become aware, our system will very naturally normalize over time. It is like when I'm driving down the freeway and notice that I'm traveling too fast, my foot will almost reflexively lift off the gas pedal, allowing the car to coast back to a more comfortable zone. If I try to overcorrect, I may create a crisis. If I continue to speed without knowing it, I may spin out of control. But my natural resilience will restore me to a more manageable pace if I simply notice and allow it to happen on its own.

How do I know when my TPMs are racing? Consciousness will deliver the message via my physical senses. I may feel anxious, edgy, irritable, or notice that I am losing my glasses when they are on my head. Feelings of overwhelm, stress or dread may call my attention to my thought-speed, or I may tune in when I realize I'm reaching for coping mechanisms like food, chemicals or shopping. However it is brought to my attention, it is far less powerful when I realize that I'm just hitting the thought accelerator, and I've speeded myself up.

LIFE AS WE KNOW IT

Somewhere in our very early years, we begin to accumulate our ideas about life. As we go through experiences and store the memories, our marvelous Information Processors translate those experiences into meaning, and we make decisions about what we like, what we don't like, what's okay and not okay, what we fear, and how well we fit in with the rest of the population. We look around us to our families, our culture, and our peers for a grasp of "the rules" (which they made up before us!) and form ideas about "how we're doing" at measuring up. We create a persona and put it on like a costume, presenting to others the picture we've created.

The more we Know, the less we Wonder. We begin to exert effort to make people and circumstances comply with the standard we have formed. We begin to measure the quality of our life by how well it fits the picture we have made up.

And the more sure we are about our meanings, the more vulnerable we are to skepticism, disappointment, and disillusionment. We "forget" that we are the ones who made up the expectation in the first place, and begin to resent that life and people aren't living up to what we thought should be. We have created a psychological prison, and we begin to gather evidence that we are right in our judgments of the "reality that sucks".

When I'm living in a psychological prison, where things just aren't as they should be, I turn again to my experience and my Information Processor, and develop ways to COPE. I become just as attached to my ideas about good ways to cope with reality as I have to my standards for good and bad reality. And I get even more frustrated if, down the line, my coping mechanism doesn't turn out to be the solution that I determined it would be.

The escape from a psychological prison often requires a major shake-up of our beliefs. Some crisis, like a near-death experience, can rearrange our thinking and we suddenly find ourselves with "a whole new outlook on life", but the simplest and least traumatic recipe for change is simply the recognition that our outlook, whatever it is, is learned and created by us, in Thought. Everything we KNOW about how life and people should be, we made up. The harder it is to see that this belief is created in thought, the more attached we have become to the belief. The more attached we become to a belief, the harder it is to recognize that it is only my thought that is stressing me out.

Life as I know it is illusory. When I've broken the code, I can discover again my own sense of Wonder.

COMING TO LIFE

In March of 2005, one of the synchronicities of my life was that I had to attend four memorial services for friends who had died within two weeks. It would seem that death was my topic of the week, and I gave it my full attention.

It is never a surprise to me that I think differently about death than most of my acquaintances, because I think differently about the vast majority of things. But this time of attention truly gave me an opportunity to look at how much of our perspective about death, and for that matter, life, is created by mankind to answer questions.

If I begin with believing, which I do, that the Mind Energy is our Source, and that each one of us is that Energy, impelled into form by its own creativity, I reflect on tiny babies and their discovery that they are alive. The feet waving in front of their faces are grabbed, and they note that these appendages appear to be attached somehow to this new Me-thing. When they cry, they can be seen to scare themselves, as if the sound comes out and registers in the hearing, the mind exclaims "What was that?!!", and eventually they discover that they can consciously make their Me-thing sound.

As babies become toddlers, and begin to experience approval and disapproval, likes and dislikes, and comforts and discomforts, they begin to form their ideas about ME. I strongly

81

believe that this is what is commonly referred to as the "terrible twos", when the infant has fully developed a sense of ME, and as yet has absolutely no sense of YOU, or anyone's reality but their own. This unhappy and distemperate age must be the most disconnected time of life for most of us.... That last severing of our previous knowledge of our union with all Energy, and the bare beginnings of our sense of living in form. We've been completely individualized, but not yet socialized, and we're furious when the world isn't going our way. Best I can figure, it takes about another eighty years to recover from this.

As we step out then into the long process of socialization, we learn about what others want; pleasing them and displeasing them, rules of society, family, and culture. We look around at the other kids, and begin to compare ourselves. Possibly we still have a strong sense of the calling and the purpose with which we took form, but we're dismayed to find that no one else cares, or honors our worthiness. The very uniqueness that we brought to life is whipped out of us by the horror of being different from everyone else, and we set aside our sense of purpose and try with all our hearts to conform.

So in a very short time, our spirits move from being fully united with the whole, to being fully self aware and separate in our individuality, to trying desperately to find a way to be part of. In varying degrees, we may completely forget that we were never, ...and never can be, ...separate.

We've created an illusion, bought it hook line and sinker, and we move through our life cycle tormenting ourselves with our own made up story.

The process of maturing, aging and dying is evident all around us, but we so completely have bought our fantasy that it won't happen to us (that for us it will be different) that we create the betrayal and tragedy around any death that touches us, as though it was never supposed to happen.

In 1993 when my father died, I remember being astonished at the physical pain I felt, and I described it as feeling like one of my life-connections in my heart had been yanked out. The bond we create with the other beings in the world that "belong" to us is still one of my mysteries. In lesser relationships, as the friends and acquaintances I've lost recently, I have more the sense of being in the middle of a game when one of my playmates had to leave ..... disappointment for myself, but no sense of sorrow for them. This casual attitude must often be kept to myself, as others with more traditional "Christian" values see me as cold and unfeeling, or at least cavalier.

But this time of intensity has clarified for me in a new way the knowing that the return to the formless, Spirit unity with the greater Creative Energy, is still totally alive in a universal sense. If I look around at a roomful of humans and see them all as the same energy propelling itself into different forms, then when one of the forms disperses, what can possibly be missing?

And if my own return to the formless is not terrifying to me, how much of life's fear does that dissolve? Indeed, what can I possibly find to be afraid of?

LIFE AS WE KNOW IT

At the most extreme example, when the terrorists made the decision to board a plane and fly it into the World Trade Center, knowing that they would be dying as well, they had to have really convinced themselves that this was a good idea. The ideas they had incorporated into their personal belief systems must have had them very convinced that we Americans were evil and must be taught a lesson.

I received an email this week that showed a film of a man picking up his computer and throwing it over the top of the cubicle onto a coworker who was annoying him "to the breaking point". Behaviors, socially acceptable or not, are always the end product of our own personal way of thinking, accumulated over a lifetime, combined with our state of mind at the time the behavior occurs.

In the study of the 3 Principles, we begin to unravel through insight and reflection the webs of thought that led us to see that our past behaviors made sense. At our worst, we can usually say that we were doing the only thing we knew to do in that moment.

Years ago I had a woman in my life whose behavior was so intolerable to me that when she entered a room I consistently found a reason to leave. I just couldn't bear to be around her! As I learned more about the Principles, I had the insight that she was being absolutely everything that she knew how to be. In a matter of weeks I had not just boosted my tolerance for her, but had truly become her friend.

Our judgments of others are always seated firmly in our ideas that they should be different than they are. One of my teachers tells us that tolerance and intolerance are exactly the same thing, just different flavors of behaviors after having judged someone lacking. When we begin to see everyone as the product of Mind, Thought and Consciousness as it is expressing in and through them and their lives, just as we are, we are in touch with the Psychological Innocence in the person's way of being. We can't and don't always let go of our own beliefs that the behavior is "wrong", but we can move beyond the idea that the person is evil, or that their actions had anything at all to do with us.

In compassion, we find someone struggling with their state of mind, with which we can always identify.

THE DRAMA OF IT ALL!

I remember the first time I was called a Drama Queen by a courageous friend who had the insight to see that I was creating huge dramas around little situations and turning it into a lifestyle. One remark by an innocent acquaintance could send me into weeks of mental stewing, hashing and rehashing what was meant and what I would say to them if I ever saw them again. When I had adequately sorted through all the details and made firm decisions on my opinions and judgments, I would then begin a verbose round of relating the story to friends who were most likely to agree with me, requesting validation that indeed I was right! As I gathered my evidence, not only did my position become stronger, but my biology would be in overload with high-drama chemicals, increasing my heart rate, causing headaches, etc.

There was a day shortly after I began studying the Principles when I was driving in my car and saw a man who vaguely resembled someone I used to know but hadn't seen in some fifteen years. As I whipped into memory about the ending of our friendship and how WRONG he had been, I became angry and frustrated all over again, and was soon gripping the steering wheel. When I noticed, and realized that I was having a violent argument with someone who wasn't even there, I had to laugh at myself. What a great demonstration of how memory and drama-making can run us in circles! I returned to the present moment as quickly as I realized what

I was doing, but it took some time for my body to finish reacting to the flood of adrenalin and who-knows-what-else my consciousness had dumped in reaction to my upsetting thoughts.

Over time as I continued "busting myself" – calling myself on how much I was making up, my mind began to give up the game. Gradually I have noticed that my thinking is quieter than I ever remember it being. Living with what is actually happening, with what I actually know, is never as high-drama as living with all the stuff I used to make up about it!

BECOME AS A LITTLE CHILD

When my grandson was a tiny infant, he would stare at me as though he were seeing my entire soul. When he could barely sit up, he looked, literally, as though he knew the wisdom of the ages. At this writing he is only four years old, but already that wisdom has become plagued with his "earthly learning". As he looks around himself at other children and has begun the human ritual of comparing himself and noticing "differences", as his intellect expands with the learning of memories, skills and data, that insightful depth of him is already harder to reach.

We associate many things with becoming as a little child – wonder, innocence, lack of judgment, and staying in the present. But what about the unspoiled access to Wisdom, Instinct, Intuition and absolute joy? I tend to forget that the access is still there, just obscured from my awareness by my "busy" thinking, which is intellect and memory-based. How different my life would be if I hadn't developed (at least) 10,000 ideas and expectations about how people should be, what they should say, what life should be like, what success looks like, what others should think about me, what they should say to me, and don't forget the ever-important how they should dress!! The accumulation of family teachings, cultural norms, and personal preferences are a virtual attic of clutter in which my wonder and serenity become buried.

In our American culture there is high regard for a mind that processes information and churns data. But often far too late we realize that we can never churn our way to the peace of mind and serenity we so desire. We cannot figure our way there. It is more a process of releasing and undoing.

In recent years there have been quite a few movies of a wide range of quality dealing with the fantasy of a memory scrubbed clean. This is not anyone's goal, as our memory gives us every skill we have for doing life, from holding a fork and walking, to performing the tasks of our jobs. But to retrieve access to our natural, peaceful, present way of thinking it can be very helpful to recognize how much mental energy we spend rooting around in our "storage" bin. Even when we are projecting the future, we are usually using stored information to imagine what is coming.

It is always possible to re-balance the scales and re-acquaint ourselves with the thought system we were born with – the one that doesn't worry, doesn't compare, and is absolutely secure in the present moment. It may take more conscious awareness to access Wisdom as we age. It's just good to know it isn't gone. It's just whispering in the chaos.

ADDICTION THOUGHTS

When looking at Addiction as a behavior that we want to change, historical models replace the "Addicted State of Mind" with a "Recovery State of Mind", with resultant different behaviors. The restructuring of our thought structures first to one of hope and possibility, then to one of non-resistance and trust, requires attention, vigilance and support. Since it is the nature of humans to have volatility in their states of mind, a priority must be kept on remaining at all times in a recovery state of mind, at least to the point of stopping short of the old behavior.

But regardless of our state of mind, we are never NOT using the Principles. What we are thinking is coming to life for us. The Principles are operating for the most hopeless addict just as surely as they are operating for the most serene guru. It is the understanding and realization of how these realities are created that (a) seems to naturally still some of the manic mental creativity, (b) puts us back in touch with the innate place of clarity and common sense, and (c) allows us to take our ups and downs far less seriously.

Trying to understand the forming of my intellect by using my intellect almost put permanent knots in my brain, but here are some of the points that were helpful for me.

When I was an embryo in mama's womb, before my brain was formed, the intelligence was already present in those cells to move forward and create a fully formed baby. It is that intelligence, at the cellular level, that always knows the next right thing to do. I am part and parcel of the Life Intelligence, and it is always available to me. This "flavor" of thought is not connected to "time" and is not connected to "dependency", i.e., it is very present moment, and has no need for anything to be a certain way in the outer world.

As I began at birth to accumulate data through experiences, storage of memories, and making meaning out of the experiences (my natural, human, creative gift of thought), I developed a very personal, unique and individual pattern of thought. My intellect develops, and I accumulate knowledge, skills, opinions, cultural norms, family norms, self-image, and memories not only of experiences, but of the meanings I made of the experiences at the time and the resultant feelings I had when the experiences happened. It is this Personal Thought that looks to the past and tries to retrofit it, and looks to the future and imagines possible scenarios. It is this way of thinking that takes the neutral actions of others and interprets them as being about us.

As I developed my personal way of thinking over the course of years, I created and became entrenched in habitual ways of thinking and behaving. I attached myself to ideas about my comfort, about how I should feel, and about how I could make myself feel better, all based on the perception of outer causes and outer solutions.

I believed that circumstances and people were causing my emotional reactions, and developed the belief that chemicals (or any other in the long list of addictive solutions) were a good solution to my emotional state. I wanted to feel better.

In the understanding of the 3 Principles, we are breaking the code regarding our own and others' mindsets, realizing that all of our struggles, be they with people, circumstances, or feelings we are having, are self-created by our ideas of what "should" be. We rediscover our natural peace of mind and inner wellbeing, and having realized that there is no "outer" problem, we no longer reach for outer solutions.

Yes, we still have bad moods. Yes, life can sometimes feel challenging. But like recognizing that the sun is not out on a cloudy day, we can recognize that we are simply in a low state of mind, and wait for the storm to pass.

A CHANGE OF HABIT

Last year I changed jobs, and the new job happened to be down the same freeway as the old one, but two exits farther. For weeks I had to consciously remind myself not to pull off the freeway on the earlier exit, as my subconscious thought was guiding me along the route it was used to. Months later, if I happened to be particularly preoccupied, I'd catch myself just before taking that 'wrong' road.

I became really aware during this period how habits of thinking live on in us long after we have made a decision to do something new and different. Whether it is an old addiction, or just an attitude that's become a way of life, it seems to be in our nature to hit the replay button unless our intention is clear and committed.

As it happened, I never did actually make that wrong turn. But I was continually amazed at how long it actually was before the road to my old job was no longer part of my thinking.

What a relief it would be to someone who is, for instance, trying to quit smoking, if they were aware that those continuing urges to smoke (long after the nicotine has cleared the system) are just thought-habits, popping through from time to time and of no particular importance. Like a freeway exit that is no longer going where we are now heading, the call of an old way could be disregarded and noticed with amusement.

CLEAR SAILING

When one of our group was unhappy with something that happened, he leapt to the opportunity to let us have it with how off-track we were, and what we needed to do to correct the situation. Everyone present jumped into the fray, voicing their opinions and defending their positions, except the few who had "issues" with conflict and just wanted to escape. I remained silent, but was intrigued with the interaction. In the ensuing days, I reflected a lot on the debate, and my own reaction to it. I had agreed with everything the man said, but I had reacted to his intensity with defensive feelings. In reflective mode, I got some clarity on my own reactions, and also on the human condition around conflict.

When my feelings look real to me, and I believe they are being caused by the outside, they incite action. I believe you have caused me to feel the way I do, and I need you (him, her, it) to change so that I can feel better.

The Truth is, the feelings are the manifestation of my own thought process, and I have been the creator of my emotional state. So the enlightened reaction to feelings, seeing them as my body's response to my state of mind, leads me back to a higher level of consciousness that brings me, usually, to clarity regarding my own reaction. Once I have reached clarity, I can communicate in a non-combative way, and my points are more easily received.

As my understanding has deepened over the years, the arrow of my life energy has turned inward. Where the Principles used to create thought which led to feelings which led to behaviors and consequences, with all of it looking real and compelling, my energy flow was outward, and I was constantly depleting myself. As I have become more inner-directed, I may wonder why I reacted the way I did and realize I was feeling insecure at the time and note that my state of mind was down and I realize the Principles, and I am renewed and continually restored. It is no longer necessary to have the outer circumstances change so that I can feel okay. By the very act of reflection I have lifted my state of mind and my reactive feelings begin to diminish. By pointing toward clarity instead of reaching for resolution, I routinely return home.

THE EYES OF COMPASSION

In varying degrees, every resentment we hold represents an action by another that we consider inexcusable, just as every guilt we hold is founded in some behavior in our past for which we can find no understanding in the present time. When we can discern some understandable reason for the action, we are well on our way to forgiveness and relief for ourselves.

So how does the phrase "psychological innocence" fit into our picture of inexcusable behavior? The dictionary definition of forgiveness is the giving up of the desire to punish. When we hold the desire to punish in our hearts, especially over extended periods of time, it eats at the vessel that is carrying it. Few will argue that discovering the ability to forgive is an enormous freedom.

When the mapping of our psychological function becomes clear to us, we can look clearly at all behavior, ours and that of others, as being the end product of the feeling state created by the state of mind at the time. We begin to realize that everyone's behavior, always, is behavior that made sense to them in the moment, in the reality they had created for themselves at that time. It is MY creative process that imagined that their behavior had something to do with me! For example, the fact that in 1959 my mother had gotten herself stressed and impatient enough to fly off the handle at me stayed in my memory for a whole lifetime. For her, she had reached her limit in a moment when I was the nearest target. Fifty years later I can clearly see that her state of mind on that day was one of frustration, disappointment, and trying to control her surroundings. I can feel sorrow for the woman who was feeling like that, and forgive in a whole new way.

There was a beautiful autumn day a couple of years ago when I happened to be in a lot of physical pain. I had a commitment that I felt compelled to keep, and was driving to my meeting immersed in self-pity and despair. Suddenly it dawned on me that in the past, when I had felt this awful, I had gotten drunk. I was touched with a deep compassion for the woman who hadn't been able to see any other solution, and would have held her in my arms and rocked her if I could. I felt a self-forgiveness in that moment that I had never before achieved, coupled with a deep gratitude that I have learned so much more about the states of mind I create so that they don't frighten me so much any more.

When we see another's behavior and recognize it as the end product of their thinking, and that the behavior makes perfect sense to them in the moment, we no longer have to forgive the behavior, we can forgive the humanness, and love the human.

COMING HOME

When I picture the clarity that I have reconnected with in recent years, the picture I like is that of an umpire, with his little broom, sweeping off home plate. Over the years, in a very natural and human way, my spiritual Home Base became buried in the accumulation of "mental debris". I still occupy the same field, and my point of clarity still becomes obscured, but I haven't forgotten where it is in a very long time, and a simple dusting off will find it always near the surface and always available.

The human condition is such a simple puzzle. We all want to feel better. Losing our way on the freeways of our creative minds is a very easy thing to do. So far, I have not conquered my humanness. I have no perpetual bliss to offer. But it's been a very long time since I've taken my own struggles too seriously, and almost never, today, do I forget where Home is....

DEAR READER:

Gaining an understanding of the 3 Principles is not accomplished through the intellect, and using words to explain them is often frustrating. But with that said, words are what we have, and in my writings I have attempted to convey the ideas that have transformed my life and the lives of so many around me. Regardless of how much information you gather, no matter how thoroughly you study these pages and the other writings available, the dawning of insight is the only way to realize these truths. So having read and learned, please point yourself to reflection, noticing as you live your daily life how the principles are at work for you. My wish for you is that you, too, will find yourself magically transformed, having "broken the code" for living.

Marilyn Wendler

6 | Life Lived And Loved

A Fine Romance

A Fine Beginning

"Here, Lieutenant! You hold this!" Her purse was swept out of her hand by the officious general, and Audrey was swept out onto the dance floor. It was the 8th of June in 1943, and as the secretary in the office where dozens of officers reported for duty every day, her presence at the officers' dance on the party boat "The Admiral" tonight had been pretty much a command performance. It was wartime, and the men outnumbered the women at any social function involving the army. At 22 she should have been excited about that, but Audrey had had to be coaxed to come at all. This had not sounded like her idea of fun!

The number ended, and the general returned her to that poor lieutenant left "holding the bag" so literally. The fashion these days was for huge purses, and hers was right in style. As she looked up to thank the handsome young officer, her stomach flipped as their eyes met, and a flash of interest sparked between them. "May I have the next dance?" His blond hair was curly, and there were blue eyes under a tall forehead that crinkled when he smiled. He scooped her up purse and all for the next dance, and there in his arms she stayed for the rest of the evening, never dancing with anyone else until the orchestra played "Good Night Ladies" and it was time to say goodnight. His friends had teased them about being so taken with each other, saying that must have been some scotch they were drinking!

It sounds like the script for a Claudette Colbert and Clark Gable movie, but it was much more real than that. The next day he stuck his head in her office, grinned, and said "I just wanted you to know, it wasn't the scotch!" Two months later, on the tenth of August, they were married. Four years later, in 1947, I entered their lives as their second daughter. To say they lived happily ever after would be to minimize the story. What they did, from that night in June until he passed away of cancer in 1993, was to show the rest of us what love is supposed to look like. What they did was set a standard for those of us who knew them that was hard to match in the real world. But it sure kept your hopes up!

When I was a child, Dad was kind of a workaholic, obsessed with doing his best and providing for his beloved and their three daughters. He had become a purchasing agent for a medical supply company, and was often known to cart home a briefcase full of papers to be worked on after supper. But supper was a ritual, and he seldom broke the habit of showing up exactly at six. So at five, the preparations would begin. Supper would be on the stove, and an air of expectancy began to develop. Mom would go in to change her dress, wash her face, and comb her hair. Then she'd cruise through the house and we'd get our instructions – "Pick up those toys, now, Daddy's coming!" or "You need to wash your face and hands before Daddy comes." And as we got older, "Turn down the music, now, your Dad'll be home in a minute." The table would be set, and everything was timed to be ready exactly at six. Then, sure enough, we'd hear his tread on the stairs, and Mom would come running to meet him. Always they closed the door and had a few minutes alone together. Always we sat down to eat as a family. And always, always, the best piece of meat or whatever was set aside for Dad.

As we grew, the constancy of their affection for each other just never seemed to waver. In the mornings they would kiss each other goodbye as if they were parting for months, and in the evenings they would greet each other as though they'd been apart interminably. Any time you walked into a room unexpectedly, you could find them cuddled up watching television, or touching each other in some nonverbal communication that children can't quite understand. They played endless games of scrabble, joined friends for bridge, were active in the church, and took us all on family outings. On Sundays we would pile into the 51 Chevy to go for a ride, and we would all sing the popular songs of the thirties and forties. To this day, I know the songs of their generation better than the music of my own day. "Don't sit under the apple tree....."

In their forties, with three daughters well on the way to adulthood, they totally sidestepped the "empty nest" syndrome when they gave birth to a son, and began a second round of diapers, tricycles and PTA meetings, complete this time with Dad coaching little league baseball.

When retirement finally came, we all watched with trepidation, thinking Dad would be lost without work. But he and my brother joined bowling leagues and golf leagues, and Mom and Dad would jump in the car and take off randomly for parts unknown. Finally he had plenty of time to be with Audrey, and he became the relaxed, easy going guy he'd always wanted to be.

I remember when I was in my forties, and went back for a visit. I wondered if my child's mind had stored memories that were unreal or imagined, and was just curious to see if my grownup observations saw the same intimacy. Sure enough, in their seventies I still found them reaching out in the mall for each other's hand, or just patting and connecting with each other at every opportunity.

Every one of their four children have been divorced at least once. I know there were times in her life when my mom felt discouraged about that, but look how high our expectations were! The poor souls we married had no idea what they were walking into.

When they celebrated their fiftieth anniversary, the whole gang of their offspring got together for a dinner party. The photos show them sitting at the head table, looking very little like that romantic young couple that danced on the Admiral. Dad's face shows the ravages of cancer, and Mom's the worry lines of fear. But they sat hand in hand, looking out at the running babies and chaos, smiling at each other, still in love. No, it certainly wasn't the scotch. Something so real, and so tangible had connected them that first night that it had never let go.

It's been ten years now since my dad died of cancer. His last words to her as she left the hospital were "We're going to beat this thing, honey!" Ten years later, she's still as much in love with him as she was then, and has never even considered dating another man. I guess, in their way, they've pulled it off! Their love survives even beyond death, and keeps on teaching those of us that knew them. I know in her heart she wishes it was the cancer they had beaten, but Holy Cow, they've beaten the boundaries of life and death. This was a fine romance!

IN OVER MY HEAD

I was born perfect.
Ten fingers, Ten toes.
Fully equipped, top of the line model.

Being the family baby
Was well within my field of expertise,
And I recall
Keeping all of my responsibilities
Well in hand.
My favorite part was laughing,
Which when accompanied by flapping arms
Brought the entire family
To rapture.

I loved it, but
The Peter Principle came early to me.

From the time I was promoted to toddler,
I was in over my head.

RE-ROUTE ME!

It took me twenty years to recover
From being reincarnated as a child.

There should be
Some alternate route
For people
Who can't hit softballs.

LOST CHILD

That poltergeist
Roaming the halls of my mind,
Slamming doors, laughing and sobbing,
Is the ghost of the little girl
Whose skeleton is buried
In the cellar
Of the house of my soul.

If she had grown up,
I think she'd have done it more wisely
Than I did.

She wouldn't have looked to cruel
Children for approval,
Or had quite so much respect
For her sister's budding breasts.
She'd have realized
That young boys' lust wasn't proof
Of her womanhood,
And that getting one of them
To put gold on her finger
Was of itself a little shallow
As successes go.

Perhaps she'd have known that making choices
Different from Mother's choices
Was an option adults have
And not a blasphemy to parental love.

She could have taught me so much
If she'd grown up.

LOST TEEN

Being popular with the Right People
Was everything to me then.
I never wondered
If I even liked the Right People,
Only prayed
That they liked me.
Having a boyfriend
Who was one of the Right People
Was a coup!
That we had nothing in common
Wasn't even an issue.

LOST DREAM

When Ronald Wallace kissed me
By the wall where the roses climbed,
I went home and wrote Mrs. Ronald Wallace
A hundred and twenty times.

When Paul Brown brought me an orchid
The night of the senior dance
I mooned for a week
At the jewelry store window
Just hoping there was a chance.

And when Sharon and Don got married
I'd lie on my bed and dream
Of their perfect life in their perfect home
And how perfect their marriage seemed.

The golden ring on a carousel
In a fantasy world we created.
How could we have helped but be let down
By a life we had so over-rated?

SADNESS

He knew when he met her
She was a cut above the rest.
He could talk to her for hours on any subject
And her laugh was a gift
Bestowed warmly and freely.
Their only fight then
Had been about her job.
Of course NO WIFE OF HIS ...
He won.
She's been a perfect wife
For all these years.
Three babies proudly raised,
President of the Women's Guild,
And hard to beat at tennis
And bridge.
But something of her spirit
Faded off,
And when they talked for hours
It was the kids,
And when she laughed
The sound was harsh somehow.
She always did what she was told,
But something seemed disquietingly
Quiet in her.
And what really pissed him off
Was how much she still looked
Like the woman he had loved.
And when she left to find herself
He hated her for not being
What she'd wanted to be all along.

WAR

Territorial rights
Over our identities
Are not governed by others,
But by ourselves.
As we've been told by experts,
The price of freedom
Is vigilance.
And protecting the boundaries
Of our souls
Must be an inside job,
Not just a good defensive posture!

Generals tell us a strong defense
Is nothing without a strong society.
It takes core pride
That can yield to love
Without yielding principles,
And a dignity in "Who I Am"
That treaties away no portion
Of the mainland.

In eulogizing our love
I realized that every time he fired a shot
I'd surrendered another bunker,
Until I had nothing left
To call my Self,
And he had no more ground
To conquer.

I AM WOMAN!

I was Superwoman once.

I jogged every morning
And threw in the laundry
Before work.

I worked all day
At a job that I loved
And made twenty seven thousand dollars.

At seven I cooked gourmet meals,
Never minded drop-in friends,
Washed all the dishes,
And laughed at his jokes.

In my spare time,
One-handed,
I balanced the checkbook,
Hired the housekeeper,
Weeded the garden,
Wallpapered six rooms
And even snaked the plumbing once
While he played golf.

During the property settlement
He told me
He never felt needed.

I DARE HIM!

A member of the frailer sex,
I'm not ashamed to be one!
If any man could keep this up,
Well, I have yet to see one.
He'd get up every morning,
Roll hot irons in his hair,
And pluck a couple eyebrows out
To make his face more fair.
Hang earrings in the little holes
He'd punctured in his ears,
And shave his legs and underarms,
O, could he persevere?
He'd have to watch his figure,
So he'd check the morning scales,
And put on make-up carefully,
And paint his fingernails.
Then off to spend a normal day
Negotiating deals.
But do it, as a final test,
Walking in high heels!

MY BABY!

There was no contract to sign
In conceiving you
That gave me even the slightest clue
That I was committing
One-fourth of my life expectancy
To your raising.
Nineteen years now since I first held you,
And I wasn't prepared at all
For the magnitude of the job.
I wasn't prepared
For the terrible twos
Or the smart-aleck sevens
Or the know-it-all nines.
If anything was harder
Than my years of puberty
It was pulling you
Through yours.
First love was agony
To endure for you.
And sending you off
To some strange campus
Took more courage
Than my first job interview
And my wedding
Combined.
But now you've really done it!
There was nothing in Dr. Spock,
or Haim Ginott,
Or even Ann Landers, to prepare me
For nineteen years of my life
Driving off on a motorcycle!

SONG FOR MY SON

No special star was shining at your birth,
And no wise man would travel to
St. Louis in July,
But you were given the power
To light the earth,
And my maternal charge
Has been in teaching you to fly.

A love for God in such a little boy,
The hunger for the church that moves you still,
The depth of tenderness
You will some day enjoy,
Are seeds of greatness you can now fulfill.

You'll find a choice at every path and turn,
A gift to give to everyone you'll meet;
A difference to be made if you will only learn
To tap your center core and be complete.
We all have heard the message all our lives
That Jesus taught, and Gandhi chose to live.

And yet the power of anger still survives,
And all the world is hungry
for the love you have to give.

So give it.
Every chance you have!
I challenge you!
There is no greater destiny to share.
If you commit your personal power
To all that you shall do,
Then each great thing
You strive for will be there.

And if you falter on this path,
And sure you will,
There is no loss, just pick it up again.
Just reach within,
You'll find the Truth is with you still,
And power of Truth will triumph
Over the seeming power of men.

GURU CAT

My cat delights in meditation time,
When she sprawls tight to me
And lets her molecules play with mine
In a symphony of form.
Her rumbling purr becomes my mantra,
And we are Life together,
All the same.
She always knew we were the same.
It was only I who thought
One greater than the other,
(Sometimes uncertain which of us it was).
She teaches me life in form,
And maybe someday I will learn
To rumble in contentment.

SUNDOWN

I took a walk last night
On a lonely mountain road in Arkansas
And the traitor sun that rocketed out of sight
Left me alone to walk in fearsome awe.
The blackest black my eyes have ever seen
Lay on the mountains thick enough to touch.
And the gravel road I followed down between
Sought out the refuge I desired so much.
Vaguely I thought of earth before Creation,
Of only me and grass and tree and stone,
A couple of birds to twitter in elation.
Never before have I felt so alone.

DON'T LOOK!

In your eyes
I see the disappointment there
In your scorn
I meet the seeds of my despair.
All the broken promises
I've made to you.
All the hope I offered
That did not come through.
All the devastation I have wrought
Shows on your face.
All the youth and hope gone
To a long-forgotten place.
I can think of only one
Solution to this pain.
I will just not chance a look
Into a mirror again.

HOPEFUL

Hopelessness.
My old familiar state
Acquired from the gate
And reinforced and grown
Till lately I have known
It far too well.

Its lessons learned
In far too many ways
And too far buried in my blackout haze,
But deeply rooted in Disease's home –
My Self, my Soul, my Life
Sees only hell.

And from the door
I stand and see her style
And see them listen to her read, and smile,
And look alert, and clap –
These people I'd avoided like a trap
Seem really quite okay.

And one by one they stand
And now I hear
That they remember all the things
That brought me here;
Have felt the hopelessness and known the hell,
And yet are here together, all alive and well,
Handing their hope to me, and saying Stay.

HOLE IN MY SOUL

I felt I'd been born
With an odd-shaped hole in my soul.
No one else seemed to have one.
Sometimes when I was very good,
They'd smile approval on me
And my separateness seemed smaller
For a while.
They said Prince Charming
Would bring Happily Ever After,
And so I waited, and looked
To every boy I dated,
And felt connected for a while.
I married young,
Being more than ready
To feel fulfillment blossom
And in his arms
My questions all found answers
And raison d'etre flourished
For a while.
I'd heard that motherhood
Fulfilled a woman nicely,
And my expectant months were filled
With expectations.
His neediness filled up my days
And yes our bond gave purpose to my life,
But wasn't quite the shape and size
To fill the hole
Deep in my soul.
War was declared to free the kitchen slaves,
And I picked up a banner
And marched off to the office
Challenging capitalism
To find the spot for me.

Prestige and income wasn't bad, for a while.
I turned to God, and tried to climb inside Him,
And hoped that He would hide me
And guide me from the hostile world.
But I couldn't maintain
Being a Spiritual Being in a hostile world.
And the world pulled me back
For a while.
I looked everywhere.
In better clothes,
New cars,
The right neighborhood.
In Paris and in London
And Lisbon.
In other men.
In other jobs.
In other cities.
Martinis helped
For a while.

I was born with a God-shaped
Hole in my soul,
That is filled not by running
From the world into God,
But by bringing my connection to God
Into the world.
By finding my connection with humanity
Through our Source.
By folding my spiritual being
Into the human experience,
And honoring both.

LET THE GAMES END

Inside the boxing ring
My old sparring partner dances,
Waving to me, Smiling, Beckoning.
In days long gone I used to hurdle the ropes
Rejoicing at the sound of every bell
And staying to the end of every bout.
I do remember faring fairly well,
Though often bloodied up a bit,
So proud of my machismo in the ring.

Somewhere along the line the losses hit.
And hit again. And harder.
And "never again" would cross my mind.
But sure as hell When I got well
I'd climb back in, Determined I could win again
But beaten always then. Still a champ inside
And nearly killed by pride That couldn't see
That he had grown too big for me.

The wounds were slower now to heal.
But all my promises "no more"
Were good for nothing when he called
And promised good times like before.
He'd wheedle in my ear: It'll be fun
No one will know I'll go easy on you
For old times' sake -- Just one?

Disease still waves and cries those
Tantalizing lies and jealously still yearns
For my return. But I have found my hopes
On this side of the ropes.
And I can't win at anything
If I don't stay out of that ring.

THE CORNER HOUSE.

It was on a corner, at the end of the road
(VERY LITERALLY!), the house where corners
Could be turned and new roads found.

The house had been rebuilt after a fire,
By a single man who knew how to cut corners,
And was waiting for his open heart surgery.
He had a dream about a home
For people who had none,
Who would become family for each other,
And make the rough corners
Of their lives an easier turn.
He envisioned them gathering at the TV,
And cooking together in the kitchen,
And laughing on the porch.

There were cats everywhere, who knew all about
The heart in the house, and all wanted
To sit on your lap at once.
The bag of cat food upended
On the stair offered easy access.
And Tommy loved
To bite the other cats on the butt
When they crawled in to eat.
I'd swear he was laughing
When he turned and ran.

The door of the corner house
Was only locked once.
But that's another story.
If anybody knocked,
We knew it was a stranger.
No one ever knocked!

There was a wood stove in the corner
Of the Corner House, and tons of firewood,
Left over from the fire.
I stared into the flames for hours on end,
And got acquainted with God there.
God lived there too.

No one kept track of how many people
Lived in the Corner House.
There were couples and kids,
Young ones and old,
Parolees and little old ladies,
And even little old ladies on parole.
When Gwen got hit by a car,
They turned the dining room
Into a hospital room,
And she lay in bed learning strength,
And giving it to others.

There was Paul who sang hymns all day
And had been a Hell's Angel.
He told stories that brought tears to my eyes
I laughed so hard,
And went with me to see the Grateful Dead,
Who were his friends.

There was Debra
Who came with her newborn baby,
and took us all to her Baptist Church
In East Palo Alto for the christening,
and we were her family.
And we all sang Amen!

There were druggies
Who never made the ranks of former druggies,

And alkies who had no yearning
For a sober breath, and midnight
Visits from parole officers, and
Dozens and dozens of people who disappeared
And left their clothes behind.
There was a registered sex offender
Who hit on all the women young and old,
And a little boy who turned
The occupants du jour
Into playmates.

And through it all
There was the builder of the corner house,
Tinkering in the garage,
Fighting to pay the mortgage,
And griping about
The incessant smell of cigarettes.
He hauled people from their beds
To take showers, threw them
Out the door to apply for jobs,
Cooked endless pots of soup, and drove us by
The Salvation Army to pick up bread.

In the moment, it never looked
Like the cozy little family life he'd dreamed of.

In the moment, it was people bickering,
And swiping each others' food,
And leaving dirty dishes in the sink.
You had to look from the distance
To see the miracles.

You had to count
The heads held high
Of people who had lived at the corner house.

Not so many as you would have hoped, maybe.
But mine. And many more.
The corners turned.
The lives made whole.
We were the dream
Of the gruff old guy in the corner house.
We are the dream come true.

THE FRAIDY FROG

She said "Be Real!" and I said, "What is that?"
A Dr. Seuss Frog hiding in a hat?
And when I reach, I come up with a hare,
And then I reach again, a dove is there!
The hopping frog avoids me as I grope
Then pauses on a stone, and gives me hope
That I can catch it yet, then flits away.
Again it leaves me, knowing what to say,
And what to do and how to act,
But having no relation to the fact
Of who I am, and how to show a me
To you that hides so I can't see!
I caught it for a moment yesterday
And stood and, trembling, gave it all away
And realized as it sprung loose once more
That it's not quite as agile as before,
And when I ask them, people lend a hand,
And watching it elude me, understand
That this young frog has all its life been kept
Deep in a hat where it survived, but slept,
Unknown, unnoticed, never exposed to light,
And now, turned loose, it hops about in fright,
Not always happy that it's finally free,
And not even always sure it's really me.
The Fraidy Frog is being merely that –
A frog that's lived
For forty fucking years under my hat!

EMPATHY

Those three little words, "I love you"
Are wonderful words to hear
But lately I'm learning three other words
That I've come to hold just as dear.
That wonderful bond of closeness
When I open up to you
The depths of my insane thinking,
And hear you say, "Yeah, me too!"

WEALTHY AT LAST

I remember a day
When wealth was finally mine.
After months of destitution
They passed the basket
And I threw in a dollar.

Enough to give away,
I truly knew
Contentment.

EXPRESSING

At morning meditation
I bring my banged up heart
And ask what is the message here?
What is my part?

This love had been a miracle!
I knew that it was real.
And now he's gone another way,
And I am left to heal.

What would you have me notice here?
What would you have me know?
Tell me the message in this pain
That forces me to grow?

This was your turning point, my child,
Let your heart's glory sing.
All of the love you've felt for him
Was an enriching thing.

Look how you were in loving him,
All that you'd like to be!
Authentic in your integrity,
Willing to simply be!

Look at the Source of all that love
You thought you were receiving.
It was erupting from YOUR heart!
YOU were the weaver weaving!

And there in your heart the love is still,
Nothing is lost to you! fill yourself up now from
Your well, and glow with the love you knew.

You can express it anywhere!
You can just wear it lightly.
Let it shine out on everyone.
NOW you are loving rightly!

Love on the express, finds its goal.
There will be one who feels it.
And until then, it lights your eyes
As you let your Source reveal it.

BACK TO NATURE

The nature of me was ready
When you came along,
To accelerate in its endless unfolding
Like the flower in fast-forward-photo
Exploding into bloom
In time-lapsed mini-seconds.

I remember first the Fear
That came with loving you
Where there had been so clearly none before.
It tangled tentacles around my heart
The more I cared.
And when you left me in April
And I had nothing left to fear,
Fear became a dead thing
With no more power in me.

And Loss moved in to roar
In all my quiet places,
Pounding like a storm of my own tears;
A Wizard of Oz impostor, making much ado,
Until the curtain slipped aside
In the vision of nothing
Of consequence missing.
The nature of me notices
That the treasure chest of a love-filled heart
Still overflowed within in all its richness –
A gift you'd left behind.
My mind's eye remembered
Men who'd loved me
When I felt nothing in return,
And that their love, poured inward on my soul,
Had filled me not at all.

The love that fed my joy, my own heart's love,
You had not taken with you when you left.
Nor could you.

And love intact, Loss starved to death in me
And whimpered on its way.

Loneliness leapt at me then,
Whining and mourning,
But finding no home to settle in
When my love's light, shining in my eyes,
Attracted friends to come and play
And dance to the music of its song;
A song of childhood,
Where Fear and Loss had left,
And loneliness could not abide without them.
The love-filled heart in the nature of me
Blew its kisses to all who saw its glow
And grew from the fuel of its own fire.

But Lord, did Lust not have its go at me!
Untouched, unkissed, she trudged around my
Brain stomping her feet in high-heeled shoes,
No less –

Crying at me that she must have her way.
Relentlessly remembering you to me,
She drove me finally to my darkest hour,
Where for a breathless month I hovered,
Wavering by the door from whence I'd come,
Thinking that I could borrow a cup of ecstacy
And slip back home
Without having been missed.
She was a fraud, dear Lust,
With empty promises.

And in the end,
From the surface where she lived,
She recognized the depth to which
My nature'd grown
And knew she was in over her head.
Sadly I kissed her cheek,
As we'd been friends once,
And wept for her, and pushed her on her way.

I belonged to Intimacy now,
Where mind and heart
And spirit walk with Passion,
And Lust can only
Play-act at its image,
Coming away empty-hearted.

The quiet settled on the nature of me,
Until the earthquake tremor
That recognized surrenders yet to come.
I turned with saddened heart to squarely face
The one who all along had seemed my friend.
And while Hope did no harm,
She made a clutter,
Nibbling as she did on seeds of lack
And leaving their shells all over on the floor.
I knew that in a way she'd kept me going,
But that somehow,
In the great Now of the nature of me
She couldn't stay.

And with a clutch at old ideas
I lunched with the December of You
And could not find the April of You anywhere
In that man's eyes.
And I said a quiet thanks

To the April of You; and Happy New Year
To the December of You; and hello
To the Nature of Me,
Shed of the last of sepals that had bound me,
Finally in full flower.

NOT THE SAME!

Tonight I kissed a man who wasn't there.
I am so used to you, sending your spirit flying
Into the meeting of our lips
To dance a pirouette with mine,
Blending our souls where the end of you
And the beginning of me
Is undefined.
He knew the mechanics just fine,
But had no clue how to unleash his spirit,
How to swirl two entities into one.
Had no clue
How to be you.

WORK AT IT!

My mind adrift on my way to work
I reflect on the job I do
And those who join in a common goal
To see a great vision through.
I think of the times we laugh and tease
While the mundane tasks get done
And the bond we feel when we get the news
That some small success is won.
Wouldn't it be just the grandest thing
To appreciate work today?
Wouldn't I find myself doubly blessed
By adding my joy to my pay!

MOTHER OF WAR

I looked my worst fear in the eye today
And saw the hollow pain that never heals
In the eyes of someone I will never know.
In the grief I pray I never have to feel.

Her son was blown apart a year ago
Doing the work that my son's gone to do,
In a place where people blow up every day
Over someone else entirely's point of view.
Today I held my worst fear in my arms
As two moms moved into a hug of pain,
And as we held each other heart to heart
She whispered to me, "Get him out of there!"
And knowing that I can't, I walked away
And found my normal poise in disrepair.

It's not my work to keep him safe today.
He's grown, he's wise, he has his work to do.
I walk. I eat. I talk to friends. I pray.
I hug a total stranger. Her grief is my grief too.

PERSPECTIVE

San Lucia boy, our eyes meet
Through the tour bus window haze,
A meeting of two different worlds,
Of all too different ways.
Shall I teach you
Of progress and a system so bizarre
That to be a better person,
You must drive a better car?
Wouldn't it be a treat for you
To see how life can be
With a microwave, a VCR and giant-screen TV?
Perhaps it is more proper that
I learn of life from you.
Will you teach me how to run so fast
Not wearing any shoes?
And how to laugh
With joy because your belly's full today?
Your simple joy, your simple life,
Is what I'll take away.

REVERSED PERSPECTIVE

Floating over La Guardia
At 15,000 feet
In a 3-D sky fathoms deep
And multi-textured.
Looking down on a matte flat world
Dull and all grey-brown.
Isn't it always
Just your point of view?

PRESENT IN WELLNESS

I look around at teachers one and all,
The bus driver
Laughing merrily through his morning,
The vice president
Scowling darkly down the hall.
Absence of death
Does not mean life at all.

The laughing in the ghetto is a song
Unheard
By bored and anxious ones
Who drive out of their way
To protect purses that hold no wealth
And cars that drive them
Further into emotional suburbs.
I sat in poverty
Looking out at my swimming pool.

The search for information taught me well.
Finding out facts can dim the darkest fear,
And there is solace in an information flow,
But more than facts are needed
If I am to Know.

And illness teaches too.
Yesterday it taught me fear of dying.
I did not like this gift.
Today I'm learning
Joy of life expressed –
The self-same gift, one might discern,
But infinitely
More pleasant to endure.

There was a day when I had neither.
No fear of death,
No joy of life,
No presence in the queue.
In flying from the face of one
I splattered anesthesia on them all.
Absence of illness
Doesn't mean wellness either.

I chastise where I've been
And navigate the course of where I'm going,
And nearly miss the holding of my hand,
The warm embrace of empathetic friends,
The butterfly that landed on my toe
While I sat writing in my journal.
Not being gone
Does not mean I am present.

PRAYER

"Know God!"
The voice inside my head declared.

But I had prayed for healing from my pain!
I asked again, thinking my Guide impaired.

"Know God!"
The voice commanded me again.

"Couldn't we have a miracle?" I beg.
I've prayed a lot, and I've been very good!
"Couldn't you just restore my healthy leg?
I'd be ever so grateful if you would!"

"Know God!"
The voice was quiet now, but stern.
KNOW resonated through me, down my spine.
KNOW may be something I will have to learn.
God isn't just the Source to whom I whine.

I can say truly that I
Do BELIEVE.
And even TRUST,
I think I'm quite a pro.
But KNOW
May be even more
Than I can quite conceive!
I cannot say I'm even close to KNOW.

Peacefully I embrace this clear direction.
Clearly I'm given somewhere new to go
Along my path of Spirit-introspection.
Surely I'll know when I have come to KNOW?

CINDERELLA SETUP!

My own Prince Charming wasn't close
To Cinderella's type of guy.
I met him when he was pushing sixty,
And he watched me for several months
To see what I was really like.
No love at first sight for him!
He squirms when I get mushy,
Razzes me about my size 11 slippers,
Doesn't dance around the ballroom,
And sends me wise-ass Valentines.
He is a happily ever after sort,
Just in a different way.
It isn't that he isn't terrific.
Just that damn Cinderella
Gave me expectations!

VALENTINE

When I think of all
The things I've lost by loving you,
I wonder that I've even stuck around!
There were parts of me
That had been there a lifetime through
That since you came around cannot be found.

For instance,
That old longing for the kind of love
That people share
For years and years and years
Is something now that I'm
Just never thinking of!
A major part of me that's disappeared!

That insecurity that used to hound me,
That knew no one could truly know my soul,
I simply can't pull off when you're around me!
Another piece of "who I was" you stole!

I used to know without a hesitation
The world was filled with younger, firmer ones
Who could displace me
Should they take the notion
With a wink and wiggle of their firmer buns!

But even strangers see how we are bonded,
And even I can't see a better fit!
So all my fears and doubts have now absconded
To leave me knowing surely, this is IT!

I don't know how to do all this contentment!
It's unfamiliar territory here!

I'm trying not to hold a deep resentment,
But I am not the same, that much is clear.

I never thought of "Happily ever after"
As being something I would ever get!
But day by day
The warmth and hugs and laughter
Keep adding up to years now since we met.

And still you flip my heart, and still I glory
In love that changes, new again and ever new.
The start of my own prince and princess story!
My old persona all dissolved in loving you.

TOUCHING

Many men have touched my hand
A few my breast
And one or two my heart

But when you open your Self to me
So that I can open my Self to you,
Without judgment,
Without fear,

The touching of our hearts
Is a touch of God.

WAITING FOR DR. WU

While waiting for Dr Wu today
In the Daughters of Charity waiting room,
I read a silly mystery,
Eavesdropped on other peoples' loved ones,
Drank seven cups
Of awful coffee,
Ate potato chips for lunch with
Fritos for dessert,
And tried to ignore that my new Higher Power
Had a shaved head
And a Fu Manchu moustache.

In another room
On a metal gurney,
My 'til death do us part' love
Floated in la-la land trusting his next move,
And by the way mine,
To people who
Had just struggled through
The rainstorm of the century
To get to work.

The windows
Of the waiting room shimmied under the wind,
The Pink Lady
Carefully inventoried her charges,
Efficiently noting that I was the one
waiting for Dr. Wu.

I didn't wonder or make up stories
About the others in the room.
They chattered endlessly about
Dr Atkins and South Beach

While 200 pounds of my life lay in cardio care
Being re-booted with something called
Cardioversion.

At noon an elderly lady announced jubilantly
That Ash Wednesday ashes
Are being dispensed in the lobby.
I felt very Protestant.

I sat wearing the ring
You gave me for Valentines Day,
The shirt I bought at the Thrift Store,
And an air of casual patience,
and speculated
On why there is no anesthesia
For the next of kin.

WHO ARE YOU TALKING TO?

How ironic
That YOUTH should leave me
In the prime
Of my life!

The years she loved me best
I was too busy
Growing up.

And now that I'm ready
To really give myself to her,
She's run off with a Navy man
Who called me Ma'am!

BODY WORK

Lifting from the couch becomes a horror show,
Bending to pick up is now an agony.
Aging is a whimper and a moan for me.
My spirit is a hottie but my body is a Model T!

I have no oomph to show up at the hot spots,
When I'm invited out I have no energy.
I can't get up and go without a hand to pull,
My spirit is a hottie but my body is a Model T!

The hunks look past me now
As though I'd disappeared.
There's more of me to love than used to be!
I flirt, their eyes roll back
As though I'm someone weird.
How is it such a hottie
Ended up in such a Model T?

My chassis has some dimples and some fading,
My headlamps lack their old utility,
My chrome is swirls of silver on my forehead,
One morning I woke up
And found my body was a Model T!

I have no antique value at the
Concourse d'Elegance,
The Body Shop can't do a thing for me.
I guess I'll throw her back in gear and putter
Down the road, the spirit of a hottie in a body
that's a Nottie, just a Model T.

NOT FORGOTTEN...

The night is warm,
The scent of flowers intense
And drifting in its pleasure
I am filled with lust,
Or something softer--
Desire.
My mind fills with the thought
Of arms around me,
Someone tall, who bends to
Kiss my mouth.
I feel the memoried response,
The hand pulling the small of my back,
I lift onto my toes
And shake myself awake.

I had forgotten, for just that moment
That I am old and gray.
No longer tall and firm
No longer slim and fiery
No longer turning heads.

For just that moment, all the systems in me
Leapt up to show me
Thought's powerful reality.
My fantasy of youth and beauty
Romance and passion,
Alive again.

HAPPY BIRTHDAY MOM!

Mom turns 85 today.
Her babies are senior citizens,
Her sweetheart is long gone,
And she takes her meals in the dining room
With her friends from down the hall.
What's the point? She cries
I have no purpose here!
Except to Mary, who's in a wheelchair
And depends on Mom to get to lunch.
Except to Lottie, who looks down on everything
And depends on Mom to point out
The other side of life.
Except to Pam, who looks to Mom
For laughter, and understanding,
And appreciation.
Except to Sharon, who looks in on Mom,
And will be sorrowful when she leaves us.
Except to all the little ones
Who get to know, as I did, what it's like to
Have a Grandma.
Except to me, who learns from Mom
Every day, that Life has purpose
In the little things
In who we are
And how entwined we are
With all the other forms of life we touch.
Except for me, who remembers far too seldom
To say wow, mom, you are something else!
Whatever will we all do
When you move on
But reminisce about how lucky we were
In this time now!

NO FEAR

In my life
I have stood at the edge of the Grand Canyon
And looked down.
I have stood
In front of 300 people in conflict with
Each other
And walked with them
Into resolution.
I have sung in front of hundreds,
Loved a violent man,
And narrowly escaped
A fatal case of self-abuse.
I have sat
Helplessly through a major earthquake
Watching all my breakables
Break.
I have held the hand of my beloved
In the Emergency Room.
I have survived without income.
Now I have kissed my son
And seen him head off for a war zone,
Honoring his decision to be there.
Tell me what else ever can I find
To fear?

BABY-BOOMER POLITICS NOT AS USUAL

You speak to our fears.
We fear.
But our fears are not the part of us we trust.
We've already seen our fears
Lead us to road rage,
And fences,
And security systems, and isolation.
We have our fears, yes,
But we long for more.
If you want to lead us, lead us to hope.

You speak to our prejudices.
We are prejudiced, we admit it.
But our prejudices
Are not the part of us of which we are proud.
We've already seen
Our prejudices lead us to slavery,
And populations in revolt
And we have learned something along the way.
We lean toward unity and understanding
And long for leadership that will take us there.
We are self-righteous, yes.
But lead us to brotherhood.

You speak to our patriotism, but we
Do not want patriotism that is a good bluff.
America represents for us the high ground.
Telling the world
They must come to the high ground
Or we'll kill them
Doesn't work.
Our buildings
And our humanness are vulnerable.

We want our integrity to be untouchable.
We know we are part of the world.
Lead us to dignity.

You speak to our faith.
But we want our faith to lead us
To a better way of living,
Not fuel our intolerance
For the ways of others.

We are a nation whose heroes are
Deepak Chopra,
And Oprah Winfrey, and Dr. Phil.
We want to be better.
Take a poll,
We will say that we want to be richer,
And we hate what the other guy is doing,
And the Good Old Days were better.
But we were THERE in the Good Old Days.

We remember when abortion was illegal,
And women were dying.
We remember air-raid drills in school,
And Kruschev promising to bury us.
We remember prejudice against females,
And Blacks, and the Handicapped, and Gays.
We remember John Kennedy's Catholicism
Being an issue.
We remember Barry Goldwater's Judaism
Being an issue.
We remember freedom marches,
And Martin Luther King,
And bra burnings,
And Dan White and Harvey Milk,
And we know that the changes have been good.

We reminisce about the good old days,
But we know in our hearts they weren't.

We want our becomings to be a source of pride.
Not what we are telling the world,
But what we are showing the world.
We want to lead the world by showing the world
It can be something better too.
We want to be led to be more
Than anything we know how to be.

We want to ask ourselves every day,
"Who are we being?
Who are we becoming?"
And we want to be okay with the answer.

Hear us cry out.
We want a
Campaign for National Integrity.

THERE'S MORE TO SEE

The little wave
Flies along to find its destiny
Reaching a crescendo as it arcs and froths
Slapping the sandy shore in joy.
"I am the mighty ocean!"
Is its cry as it descends.
"Can it be done so quickly?"
Is its whisper in the end.

The tiny twig
Above the canopy, pushes a leaf to spread,
Joyous to be a part of Spring again,
Soaking the sunlight, feeding the branch below.
"I am the mighty sycamore!"
it sings to morning,
The roots and trunk
beyond the world it knows.

The foolish poet
Hears inspiration bursting to be written,
Writes as he must, before the stanza fades,
Swells in accomplished genius on the page.
"I am Creative Mind!" the vain will glory,
Only the scribe, an image of the sage.

INNERCIRCLE PUBLISHING

Catalog of Original Titles

ISBN	Title
0-9720080-9-8	the sometimes girl by Lisa Zaran
0-9720080-5-5	A Metaphysical Interpretation of the Bible by Dr. Steven Hairfield
0-9720080-2-0	Return To Innocence by Dr. Steven Hairfield
0-9720080-3-9	Interview With An American Monk by Dr. Steven Hairfield
0-9720080-4-7	Interview II: Heath and Healing by Dr. Steven Hairfield
0-9723191-4-X	Poetry to Touch the Heart and Soul by Marla Wienandt
0-9755214-9-7	Touched by Spirit by Marla Wienandt
0-9723191-8-2	Stress Fractures by Andew Lewis
0-9723191-6-6	Life Rhymes by Rene Ferrell
0-9723191-7-4	One Hundred Keys to the Kingdom by Prince Camp, Jr.
0-9723191-0-7	the voice by Rick LaFerla
0-9755214-0-3	On the Edge of Deceny by Rick LaFerla
0-9723191-5-8	A Day in the Mind by Chad Lilly
0-9755214-6-2	uncommon sense by Chad Lilly
0-9755214-7-0	Peace Knights of the Soul by Dr. Jon Snodgrass
0-9755214-1-1	Petals of a Flower by Patricia McHenry
0-9755214-2-X	Poetry-Prose-Stories by J.L. Montgomery
0-9762924-0-8	The Weave that Binds Us by Martin Burke
0-9762924-2-4	Dare to Question by Jack Perrine
0-9762974-2-6	The Twelve Mastery Teachings of Christ by Lea Chapin
0-9762924-3-2	Alnombak by Ken Delnero
0-9762924-7-5	Life is a Song Worth Singing by Clarissa LeVonne Bolding
0-9762974-3-4	The Spirit Within by Susan Marie Ratcliffe
0-9720080-8-X	And the Angels Spoke by Rebecca J. Steiger
1-882918-00-2	From Ashes To Angel Light by Rebecca J. Steiger
0-9762974-6-9	The One Minute Miracle by Daniel Millstein
0-9762974-5-0	Unemployed: A Memoir by Reginald L. Goodwin

Are You Aware?
www.innercirclepublishing.com